The Hummingbird's Garden

A Collection of Poems

The Hummingbird's Garden:

A Collection of Poems

by Jill Tyler-Dolan

The Hummingbird's Garden

Copyright © 2024

Jill Tyler-Dolan

All rights reserved. No part of this book may be reproduced in any manner without the consent of the author.

Written and illustrated by Jill Tyler-Dolan

Paperback ISBN: 9781738919123

Author Website: jilltylerdolan.com

Dedications:

This book is dedicated to my beloved Grandma. You have always been a big supporter of mine. I'm so lucky to have you in my life. Thank you for inspiring me, and, most of all, thank you for loving me. I love you so much. You are so important and special to me. *The Hummingbird's Garden* really is inspired by you. I hope you enjoy it.

This book is also dedicated to my uncle, John Weese, who passed away before it was published. You were so looking forward to reading my book, and it means a great deal to me that everybody who reads this will know how special you were. I love you, Uncle John. You will forever be in my thoughts.

Planting Seeds - Page 1

Grandma's Garden

Finding Joy

True love vs. New Love

A Conversation Between Mind and Future

The Road to Nowhere

Meaning of Success

Imagine

Take Action

Life's Treasures

Change

Hear Me Roar

Winds of Change

Routine

Emotion Before logic

Embracing Myself

Free Birds

Community

Unspoken Language

Self Love

Why You Hate Poetry

You Are the Future

Loud Reflections

Making a Difference

The Loudest

In Love

In My head

Growing — Page 29

Déjà Vu

Megaphone

Solitary Walk

True Colours

Die Without Regrets

Chasing the Ghost of Perfection

You Are the Greatest

Growing Up

Childhood

Her vs Me

Broken Things

Dreams

Clear Skies

Light of the Moon

Gather Around

Fight For, Not Against

I Will Not Conform

Raising My Voice

Human Nature

Change Has Enemies

Fight with Arrows of Love

As I Am

Pain Exists for Everyone

My Strength

Changing the Norm

Growing

We Are All Human

The Mountain

Going Home

Standing in My Own Way

Release

Shielding Emotions

Weeding – Page 67

Don't Be a Bystander

Bridge to Success

Judgement Day

Worth

I Know Pain

Life Is an Adventure

Escaping Reality

The Insignificance of Scars

Barbie Doll

Fairytales

Education

On the Shoulders of Giants

The Friend Whose Name I Forgot

My Burden

Our Planet

My Arrows

Who am I?

Generosity

Weeding

DJT

The Darkness Within

Love Hurts

Labels

My Mirror and I

The Talk

Pale Hands

Beast

Breaking the Mold

Training Day

The Chains We Wear

Are You Okay?

Dreams vs. Reality

Black Storybook

Cage Fight

Save Your Tears

Blossoming - Page 108

Beautiful Girl

Diamond in the Rough

Good Vibrations

Success is Not a Ladder

My Beauty's Been Earned

The Light She Gives

Watch Me Burn

I'mpossible

IV

Blossoming

The Warrior in Me
The Hummingbird's Garden
Grandma's Kitchen
Herstory
Happiness
Life is a Blessing
God's Art
Welcome to High School
In God's Arms
My Best Friend Lily
Being Myself
Disneyland
Meditation
True Beauty
Reminiscing
Pain Does Not Discriminate
I Love Myself
Black Goddess
I Am Woman
My Garden
A Love Letter to Vancouver Island
Rainbows
You Are a Diamond
The Birth of a Goddess
Exhibit of Joy
The Hummingbird's Song
Building My Own Table
Family
Uncle John

Chapter 1:
Planting Seeds

Grandma's Garden

My Grandma's garden
Is my happy place.
She nurtures it
And cares for it
Just as she cares for
Each of us.
The flowers thrive
And grow,
Reaching to the
Light, and bathing
In her love and
Uplifting spirit.

Finding Joy

Where did Joy go?

Did she run away?

Has she escaped from our grasps

So we understand

We do not deserve her?

Has she decided to

Leave the hearts of

Everyone who claimed her

As their own?

I'm on a quest

To find Joy.

Although I've met her

A few odd times,

I miss her dearly,

And wish to welcome

Her home.

True love vs. New Love

How do you tell

The difference between

True love and new love ?

Is true love supposed

To last forever ?

Is new love supposed

To wither and die

Like a flower burnt

By the sun's rays?

They say the first love

Is the truest of all,

But that love is new too

Maybe it's easier to ignore love

Altogether—

True or new,

Fake or old—

Because I can't tell the difference.

A Conversation Between Mind and Future

Future

What is it you want from me?

I am only a Mind

Trapped inside a shell.

The way I spin

Is like a hamster on a wheel.

I can go forward in order to have

A person dream and hope and wish

Upon a ball of dust and fire

Billions of light years away.

You ask me to only look forward

Towards you, Future,

But I can't ignore the rest of me

Because without the help of Past,

You would not exist.

Understand I must spin backwards

Sometimes, just as a clock moves backwards.

Past is a substance.

Past is *something*.

But you,

Future,

You cannot be seen from afar

Cannot be heard by another shell

And cannot be released

Because people would fear us.

Please understand—

Like you, I am complicated.

I not only spin back and forth,

But I spin side to side, up and down

I suffer the chains that society

Burdens me with.

What else do you want from me?

I am only a Mind.

Like you, I am nothing,

But I am also everything.

The Road to Nowhere

Some days,
It feels like
We've changed,
Like we've grown.
Then there's
Those days when
It feels like
We are still in
The same place
As we started
And we're trying
To move forward
Against the biting wind
And against ourselves.
We're stuck on a treadmill.
The road that
Could have been
Doesn't exist;
It was only an illusion.
And we kept walking along that
Road that led to nowhere
For the convenience
Of the people
Who told us
We were moving forward —
The oppressors —

But they don't have
Us fooled.
We've learned to
Build our own roads ,
To rise above our challenges.

Meaning of Success

My fear was that
I was never going to be
Worth anything.
 I thought that success
Was the way to
Fill the empty hole
That I believed I was,
But I knew that, as long as I
Had love in my heart
And had people
Who had love for me,
I was never going to be
Worthless.

Imagine

Imagination:

The risk I'm willing

To take any time

And any day.

How would

People dream or create

If it weren't for

That which doesn't

Yet exist?

Take Action

You're angry,
But you do nothing about it.
You're hurting,
But you cry in silence.
You wish things were different,
But don't want to
Put in the effort to change them.
Ignoring what's going on
Is no longer an option.
Use the gift of your voice
So that you can be heard,
Be seen, be listened to!
Now is not the time
To stand in the background,
Blending in with the wall.
The power of change
Lies within you—
Use it.

Life's Treasures

The things I took for granted,
Treasures that blew away with the wind—
I watched them disappear.
I thought the beauty of my life
Would be infinite,
That my life was my property.
Now, I treasure every passing
Moment, memory, second ,and year.
I cherish every smile,
Every laugh that bubbles
From my loved ones,
Every long walk,
Each hard discussion and special moment,
Because I know that,
Like the wind,
Life can change
In an instant.

Change

C-H-A-N-G-E

Change

The word challenges you

You either hate it

Or you love it

I've yet to meet

A person who's

In between

Some want to fight it

Some choose to embrace it

To some, it's an old friend

Change

C-H-A-N-G-E

Hear Me Roar

Isn't it funny how words
Can sit still and silent
On a page?
Until you read them...
Then they seem to be
As loud as a lion's
ROAR,
Sending messages to you.

Winds of Change

You can't sit and
Wait for the winds of change
To come to you.
I've done that;
Sometimes, you have to
Turn on the fan
And create your own breeze.
Silence will do you no good;
It will be
The death of you to wait
For change without saying a word.
You can't be silent and expect to be heard.

Routine

Routine:
More than just a word.
I see routine every day
In people simply
Going through the motions
Of their lives.
It possesses people and
Makes them forget to feel.
They begin to hear and
Not listen,
Talk without communicating.
They speak to their cell phones
As they stumble down the street.
Ah, routine...
A world without colour
Can't anyone who has a routine
Just stop? Stop.
Stop and take in all the colours
And beauty of this world.

Emotion Before Logic

Emotion before logic

That's how I think.

I put myself where the other

Person is standing

And walk beside them for

A little while,

On the pebbled roads

Over the grueling hills

Through the mud

And in the meadows

Feeling every feeling they feel

Every hurt, every pain

The joy, the happiness

Emotion before logic

Embracing Myself

I let myself go

And when I realized I'd lost her

I rushed to get her back

She'd been neglected

And misunderstood

And she wandered a ways

Away from me

But when I finally found her

I embraced her

I let myself go

But now I'm found

Free Birds

Flap flap

Go the bird's wings

As I stand and watch

Pitter patter

Falls the rain

From the gray sky

Leap, leap

Bound the deer

Into the thick forest

I long for something

They all have

Freedom

Free to fly

Free to fall

Free to leap

Into the unknown

Freedom

Flap flap

Go the bird's wings

Community

I want to see

One united planet—

See the beauty in one another,

See the beauty in embracing each other

And standing together

As one connected family.

That is community.

Unspoken Language

Silent whispers

Muted screams

Quiet shouts

Piercing nothingness

Words tumbling out

Of sealed lips

Loud secrets

Eyes saying more

Than mouths

Ever could

Words unspoken

Voice broken

Voice has become

A jumbled mess

Lost in a world of chaos

And taken for granted

By many

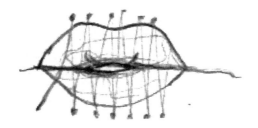

Self-Love

At some point
Someone told me
Self-care and self-love
Were selfish.
They acted like
It was some sort
Of crime to
Look in the mirror
And say, "I look bomb today."
I've learned since then
That self-love isn't selfish.
In fact, it's the opposite;
It's hard to love others
If you hate your reflection
Instead of loving who you are.
So really, self-love
Is actually selfless;
I love myself
So that I can love you.

Why You Hate Poetry

Pointless, stupid words

On a dumb, blank page,

Like the meaningless garbage

That spews from politicians' mouths,

Flowing from left to right.

They really expect you to absorb this stuff?!

Poets add fluffy words

To surround their true messages,

Then... expect you to decipher it

Embrace your inner Einstein;

Why do you hate poetry?

Because you do not understand it,

And people hate what they cannot understand.

So maybe, if you could,

You'd grow to love it—

Or, you know, forget it

And assume that there is

Nothing in this world more

Ridiculous and stupid than

Poetry itself.

You Are the Future

"You are the future"
Is the slogan
They use to
Inspire us to change the world,
But one could argue
That my future is not
The future.
I've got nothing to do
With the change to come,
The change we've
Lived and died for.

I suppose the past
Is the future
If you let it be,
With the same stories being
Seen and heard and told,
But I guess maybe the present
Is also the future
Because it is the very
Bridge we cross from
Past to future.
You know, maybe we're all the future;
It can't all happen in one generation.

Loud Reflections

I talk about mirrors
Because they've been
A friend and an enemy;
They scrutinize my every flaw
But bring out my beauty. I hate them,
I love them,
Because in a world
Full of twisted lies,
Mirrors give a
Backwards truth.

Making a Difference

It's not worth

The fight

It's not worth

The hassle

It's just not

Worth it

If people choose

To do nothing

About an obvious problem

It sure as heck is

Worth something

It's worth something

To people who can't

Do anything to

Create the change alone

It's worth it to me

It's worth it to you

I'll accept the fight

The hassle

I'll accept it all

If it means

I've made a difference

The Loudest

They say,

"Actions speak louder

Than words."

And I think actions

Don't really have

A choice, especially since

Words are so darn loud,

Desperate to be heard over the silence.

In Love

I have no desire to
Fall in love
The pain is
Too much to bear
But I will write love stories
And make up memories
About the many times
I have

In My Head

It frightens me;
You know how I am the
Only person on this earth
Who can truly understand me.
No one else will know
What I think,
Why I think,
How I think,
They watch a body live,
Not knowing where it's been
Or where it's going.

Chapter 2:
Growing

Standing in My Own Way

I kept putting off my life

Waiting for the perfect time

The perfect moment

To begin the adventure

Only to realize

That perfection is a myth

Pain Exists for Everyone

Inside this home

Is a wealthy young lady

Who has it all

Pearls rest upon her neck

The finest faux fur surrounds her

As she complains about

A purse she lost earlier

While she warms her feet by the fire

Not far from her home lies

A homeless man

Thankful and joyful

Just to receive dinner that night

The man normally goes to sleep hungry

And the lady cries herself to sleep

Tortured by the deaths of

Everyone she loved

He's an optimist

She has extreme depression

Different situations

With very different problems

Die Without Regrets

Sometimes I wonder
Why I bother to do what
I know is good,
Because you can be
Kind, compassionate, and caring,
But life will still
Slap you in the face;
People will still hurt you.
You could be the most
empathetic person in the world
And still be
Knocked down,
Stabbed in the back,
Hated, and treated like dirt
By people who
Don't even know you,
People who judge you
Based on the shell
That carries your soul.
They don't want to
Get to know that soul,
But the reason to do good,
Les within you.
It's a choice you make,
Whether or not you
Want to die

Knowing you could have done
Better while you
Had the time.

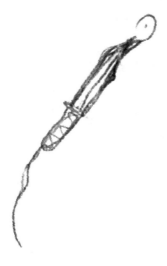

Changing the Norm

I know you see it
Just as I do;
The problems of our
World are no secret.
Even worse are
The people who say,
"Things are how they are
Because they are."
Worse yet, are
The people who believe
They may have a solution
But choose to sit back
And twiddle their thumbs,
Hoping someone else will
Take action instead.
Beyond that
Are the people who are
Too afraid to stand out.
They don't want to stand up
And shout,
"I have an idea that could
Improve this world!"
But believe they will
Be seen as strange.
To that, I laugh and say,
"No normal person ever did

Change the world."
The world has been changed by
Normal people denormalizing
What was considered normal.
What everyone else accepted,
They rejected and said,
"Action needs to be taken."
Be the person who takes the action
For the better.

The Mountain

I speak the words

Of the ones who

Inspired me before

I was even considered a person.

They all climbed a mountain —

This mountain

We call life —

And they left me footholds and handholds

So that I too, could climb it.

On this mountain,

You encounter

Brutal bears,

Killer cougars,

And slithering snakes,

You cannot trust them.

The cougars always

Watch you from afar,

Waiting to pounce on you and

Knock you down

In the hope that you will

Never get back up.

You simply can't

Escape the bears;

They chase, climb, swim, slash;

They bare their teeth

And cut into your existing scars.
I've only climbed an
Eighth of this mountain.
I've encountered the
Snakes, cougars, and bears,
But even they can't stop me.

Release

I let go of the

Burden that wished

To tie me down forever

Now I'm floating, floating

In the clouds

I see colour

I see light

I am free

Megaphone

I pick up my megaphone.
They say that it's a human right to speak,
That you have freedom to a voice,
A voice to say *yes or no*,
I don't like this, I don't like that.
Then they put a bullet into
Your head to silence you.
Their hatred is like the blood
You let out of a wound.
What about the freedom to be
Listened to?
Non-existent! So-called powerful people
Have the privilege to talk.
You see?
The freedom of voice
Truly only exists for the fortunate few.
I shout through my megaphone
As I stand upon my mountain
But my words are simply dead,
Just as those of the people who used their
voices before me.
You know, having a voice
Is supposed to be freedom,
But sometimes it feels like it's no less restricting than
The bars of a prison cell.

The megaphones of the people before me
Are covered in blood,
And their blood is on the hands of people
Who could have listened,
But instead chose to silence them.
I drop my megaphone.

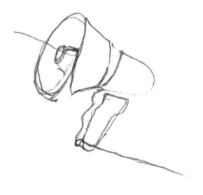

Light of the Moon

Your words are like a knife

In my back

The hit me

Like a heart attack

Your words pierce

Through my skin

And I wonder what you've

Been hurting from

They say that hurt people hurt people

I hope you get better soon

If you need hope

Look up at the moon

Even she shines

In the darkest hours

Why can't you?

I Will Not Conform

I was too much

Then I was too little

I was too large

Then became too small

Too young, too dumb

I've heard it all

I was just too over the top

But I wasn't going to change my soul

To make others around me

Feel more comfortable

Creativity

It's impossible.

That is,

Until you make it possible.

Chasing the Ghost of Perfection

I gave up on

Trying to be perfect

Perfection was

Never achievable and

I grew tired of

Chasing a ghost

A speck of dust

A breath of air

I gave up on perfection

But I learned to fall

In love with my imperfections

You Are the Greatest

If they don't like you,
If they choose not to
Get to know you,
If they judge you
Based upon snapshot,
If they choose to hate you,
If they betray you,
Treat you like garbage,
And turn their backs on you,
Maybe they're not worthy
Of your greatness.

The Power of Nothing

I used to think of myself
"I'm nothing."
But slowly, slowly,
I began to realize
That, by my own definition,
The universe started out
As nothing
And it created the world. It led to life;
It created you and I.
And if that is
The result of nothing,
There is more
Power within me,
Within us all.

Déjà Vu

I was running away
From her, looking
Behind me as I
Sprinted faster and faster.
She represented
The things that I did not.
She believed in
Things that I did not.
Even try to believe in
Or agree upon.
Suddenly, I ran into something:
A mirror.
Turns out it's
A lot harder to
Run from your
Reflection than I'd thought,
Even if it is an
Old one.

Fight For, Not Against

With so much

Going on in the world

I think we see

So much to fight against

That we forgot that

In the beginning

We were fighting *for something*

The purpose was to build and rebuild

Not to tear down and destroy

Fight *for something*

Fight for a lot of things

But never forget

How it all started

Solitary Walk

I had to disconnect to connect.
I had to see past what was being said,
Getting up day after day,
Living for the sake of others.
I had to let them go
So that I could get to know myself,
Start to love myself.
So I took a walk,
A long walk,
Alone, it was a moment of solitude.
I had let society control me.
It had built a mold for me before
I had even come into being
I had to disconnect from society,
So I could connect with myself.

Her vs. Me

Sixteen years before

I had grown to love her

She was untamed

And seemed to use every

Means necessary to

Work against me

I was tempted to give up on her

She was just too wild

For a girl who

Was already living in

Eternal chaos

But I finally fell

In love with my hair

She still drives me crazy sometimes

But every curl, coil, and kink

Is placed perfectly

Making me proud to be black

And that makes me beautiful

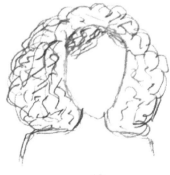

Broken Things

It took me a while

To realize that even

Broken things

Can be healed

With a lot of love

And some time

That's how I healed

And how others do too

True Colours

I covered my mouth
With my gloved hands
I wore all black
So I could hide my true colours
My true identity
But now I let them shine
Through me
Radiating into my world
I see shades of purple

Shielding Emotions

I felt the need to
Protect my emotions,
Because, while they hold power,
They can also be used
As a weapon.
I must understand
Who I am trusting
To understand them.
But I've found those people,
And when you do,
Never let them go.

We Are All Human

Unity—

It's what makes community possible,

But there is so much

I see

That drives us apart.

Division

Is so embedded in our culture;

Labels are thrown at us;

Stereotypes are meant to define us.

Sometimes I wish I could say,

"Stop! That's enough!"

Take someone's hand,

Feel their skin against yours;

Feel the softness and folds and lines of their palms.

Does it really feel any different

Than your hand?

Look into their eyes—

Really look at them

See the colour

Are they made differently

Than your own eyes?

We are all human.

We are all one community,

One world.

Childhood

With all that I've become now

I wonder why I doubted

My younger, more naive self

Because all she's did

Was lead my to my own

Greatness

Gather Around

You ever notice how
People can despise each other,
But when they sit down
And have a meal together,
They come together?
Like music, they harmonize
And understand each other .
Feast for food, feast for friends.

Growing Up

Do you remember when the world felt big?
When 1,000 miles felt like 1,000 days?
Do you remember when the
Smallest things were enough
To put a smile on your face?
I remember when my problems
Were like melting ice cream
Gone in a day.
Now, my problems are larger
And they last for longer.
And I remember when I knew
That I was enough,
But now all that has changed,
And I'm worth less and less
As I grow older.

Going Home

I never wanted to go back to
That lonely island
I was on
But everything I lived through
And everything I felt
On the island
Made me stronger
The tears were shed
Fears were set in
And I had no choice but
To face everything that
Invaded my mind, body, and spirit
I geared up, with my armour
Tight to my skin
I became fearless
I took my sword,
And defeated those alien
Thoughts and feelings that had taken my
Body over for years
I then built my boat
Using everything I learned on the island
And I sailed home
I was finally free

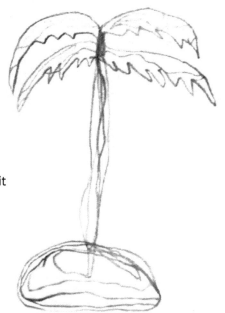

Change Has Enemies

Don't be afraid
To make some noise
Break some glasses and
Shout at the top of your lungs
Silence is the biggest
Enemy of change

As I Am

I know who
I want to become
But I'm wise enough
To know that
I first have to love myself
As I am

My Strength

I became stronger

When I realized that hating others

Isn't power or strength

It only festers and consumes you

Loving people sets you free

So I no longer hate people

Because no one deserves

My energy and attention

If they don't give me theirs

Human Nature

I was afraid of being vulnerable
Of letting more of me be known
Afraid of showing emotions
But sometimes
It's just not enough
To be tough
Sometimes you have to show
That you're human

Raising My Voice

I was quiet.

Afraid to make noise,

Wishing for change,

Hoping for better,

Praying for light and peace.

Now, I make noise.

I'm no longer silent.

I realize that noise

Can create change.

Fight with Arrows of Love

As long as you fight with

The poisonous arrows

Of hatred

You will lose every

Single battle you're in

Perseverance

Though the tears kept falling,
I knew that,
If I gave it some time,
If I gave my life some time,
Better days would come.

Dreams

The lessons of life
Are a blessing.
The toughest may
Be learning to love me.
Having those dreams
And goals for my
Future self, and loving
Who I was going to become,
Was where the self- love ended.
But now, I love myself as I
Am today, still dreaming about
Tomorrow, but embracing
Myself as the masterpiece
I am.

Clear Skies

Blowing away the dark clouds

That have plagued me for decades

Was so liberating

I knew that I had grown into

My own strength

It had been there all along

I just needed to unleash it

Chapter 3:
Weeding

Breaking the Mold

The world has its own

Set of molds

Lines drawn that I couldn't cross

Boundaries and walls in between

Creating a labyrinth I had to navigate

To get to the end

Would be impossible

It's different for each person

The man next to me has a couple of hot rocks to walk over

To complete his course

My path includes land mines

Traps, and poisonous snakes

That's why I've got to break the mold

And chart my own path

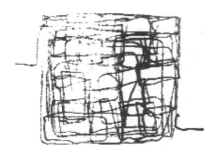

Bridge to Success

You walked upon us

Over your bridge to success

Tears and sweat run down our faces

We gave up so much

Unwillingly,

And all you gave was a smirk,

A wave, and a "see yak...never."

And as you walked over the bridge

You slapped us in the face

And beat what little pride

We had left, out of us.

Then you asked later,

"Why are you angry?

We've made progress.

We've done well.

Stop being angry over things

That no longer exists."

But you see?

We're not angry,

We're tired.

And if there had been real change,

We wouldn't need you

To tell us about it.

We no longer have the

Energy to display the hate

That you poisoned us with.

We're tired of being stepped on,
Bruised, and beaten,
Tired of smiling and saying
Everything's okay.
It's not!
We're tired of the separation,
Tired of the hate and discrimination,
Tired of our skin being a tattoo
Marking us as less
Than human to those around us.
We just want a bridge that
We, too, can walk over
Rather than being the bridge
That is walked upon.

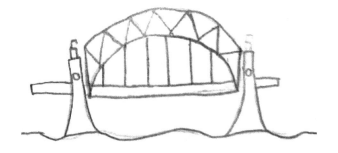

On the Shoulders of Giants

Dragged through a current

Of a river we never wanted

To step into

Our heads go underwater

And as we try to step out to breathe

A foot pushes us under

Suffocating us with waves

That seem to steal the oxygen

That we fought so hard

To let in

Over the years

Many have battled

And many have perished

So that I, a black girl

Can be empowered

To do anything

The power to be educated

To be a creator

And to earn wealth

In every sense of the word

DJT

The opportunity arose
For me to change
What I had said,
To take back the
Words of hatred
My tongue had let me form.
But, no;
I did not.
I weaponized my voice,
Flexed my privilege
Upon the less fortunate,
Upon the silent,
Upon the dependent,
Because I am their leader
And they will follow
And hang on my every word.
That is what will make them
Fall off the cliff
To their deaths —
Because I shoved them
With the power
Of my voice.

The Beauty in the Mess

When I think of life,

I think,

"What a mess."

If anyone says

They have their

Life completely together,

They are either lying,

Or God has blessed them

Beyond belief.

Please, don't clean up

This mess. I need to

Embrace the beauty of this mess,

The beauty of my life,

The beauty of not having my life together.

And sometimes being a walking,

Talking wreck.

Embrace the beauty in the mess.

Forgotten Years

I want to forget those years.

And yet, at the same time, I don't.

You know that internal debate

You have when the

Series of experiences that

Broke you, and tore you up,

Was also the ones that made you,

And built you up?

Those years are still in my head,

And I still don't know

If I want to

Let them go

Or hold them close...

The Talk

Keep your hands visible
Look into their eyes
Smile and nod
Do exactly as they say
Don't make any sudden moves
In fact, don't move
Unless you're told to
We learn what to do
With the police at a young age
We learn that if you make
One false move
You could end up dead
Why is that
I wonder
When we are just as human
As the next person?

My Arrows

I shot arrows
At the ones I loved
The most of all
I pierced their hearts
And left them to fade
Away in the dark
And when I awoke
They still embraced me
With loving, open arms

The Insignificance of Scars

I bop to my music

As I stroll down the street,

Feeling the beat

In my every step.

When I reach the intersection,

I decide to turn left.

The music stops

And I'm faced with one of

My many fears:

A mirror.

Not just any mirror,

Oh no, but

A mirror that

Zooms in on my every flaw—

Notices the extra pounds here,

The stretch marks there,

The scars that mark my body.

It shows the dark circles around my eyes,

My every insecurity.

Even worse,

It shows my past.

Tear stains against the glass,

The blood and the anger,

The pain.

My silence shatters the mirror;

The sound is deafening.

My music begins again,
But I am haunted by
What I saw.
Not that I've never seen it
Up close like that was awful
Yet I realize how insignificant
Flaws really are
When you have so much
More to offer.

Labels

White, Black, Asian:
Every word strikes me
Like a leather whip.
They beat me.
Rich, poor, homeless;
Labels used to describe us,
Words said to divide us
And make us less alike.
Beautiful, pretty, ugly
Each word created to
Make me forget
I'm human.
Like a leather whip,
Labels beat us all down,
But in the end,
We are no less than human
And no more than each other.
We're different, but the same
In many ways.

Barbie Doll

Barbie was a perfect
Representation of beauty
According to society
Long blond hair
Pencil- thin body
Bright blue eyes
But me
I was the complete opposite of Barbie
Dark skin, dark hair
Dark eyes compared to
Her pretty blue ones
In my whole collection
There was one black doll
The rest were pretty white ones
All my friends
Wanted to look like her
But I knew I couldn't
And that was when I realized I was "ugly"
I accepted I would never
Be pretty like Barbie

Judgement Day

I wonder
If, 10,000 years ago,
People looked at each other
And automatically decided
To hate each other.
I wonder
If the first thing they truly saw
Was the amount of melanin
In someone's skin.
I wonder
If they asked you
What your job was in order to
Get an idea of your wealth,
To decide if you were worth their time
I wonder
If people were willing to
Kill each other
For power over a nation.
What I really wonder is this:
When was it that people turned on one another,
Decided it was easier to hate than love,
Or even tolerate
When did they decide that
What you had between your legs
Determined your place in the world and
Whether you were capable enough

To succeed and make it in life?
What I wish is that people
Would judge others on
Who they are and
Who they choose to become,
Because character far outweighs
In value to
The colour of your skin,
Your gender,
Your sexual orientation,
Your outer beauty,
Or any other shallow thing
We use to measure
A person's worth.
Character is what matters.
And the fact that each of us is human
Is what matters.
Love matters.
I wonder
When we forgot that.

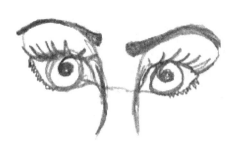

Education

"Explain slavery to me,"

The teacher says

And because I wasn't

Going to get paid

To teach the class

I left my lips

As they were

Still, unmoving.

Multiple pairs of eyes

Rested upon me

With unmistakable pity

Something I couldn't understand

Those slaves risked

Everything so that 155 years later

This black girl

Could be among these students

Preparing to graduate

Where they felt pity

I felt pride

At what we've accomplished

And how we're still fighting

For everything we deserve

So I put my disdain

For the teacher behind me

I opened my mouth

And I taught the class

I Know Pain

I know pain.
I go to school with a smile on my face
And, as soon as I step through the
Door of my house, I replace
It with the frown I've been
hiding all day.
I know the pain of
Trying to keep my head up
When gravity pushes it down
Of trying to scream and be heard
When my head is underwater,
My struggle to breathe heard only by me
I know the pain of not knowing,
Not understanding,
The pain of asking why, why, why
And receiving only silence for an answer.
I know the pain of hating, and being hated in return,
So I surrendered
I know hate, I know pain
And I surrendered so that I could love.
To every person that
Pushed my head down
To the water that silenced my voice,
To the people that made me feel weak:
I love every single one of you.

Because hate destroys,
I don't know what the future holds,
But here's what I do know
I will love! Not because I'm weak,
But because I'm strong

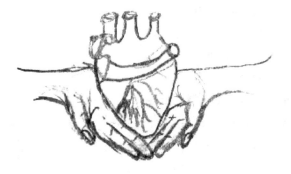

Life Is an Adventure

Do you think that
If I were rich,
I would never be sad?
That if I were beautiful,
I would never be betrayed?
Maybe if I were kinder,
I would never get hurt,
Or if I were thinner,
I would never be depressed.
If I could be perfect,
Would I miss out on adventure?
I see now that nothing—nothing—
Can shield you from the battles of life.
The journey is what makes it so special.

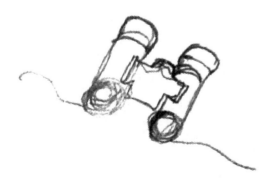

Love Hurts

Love is supposed to be

A gentle caress,

A warm hug,

A tingle on the lips.

But if that's true,

Why does love hurt,

So darn much?

My Burden

I wanted to let go

I just didn't know how

Even if the burden

Was dragging me down

Our Planet

We're killing the world
For the benefit of one species:
Us; humans.
People like to
Talk about how
Smart they are,
But I can't help
But think
We're really stupid.
We have a planet to
Live on
And we murder it.
Except, after *this* murder,
There will be no trials,
Only further death.

Training Day

There's a pencil mark
Up there on the wall
About ten feet up.
I've trained every
Day of my life to
Be able to jump up
And reach it
I have tried and failed
Time and time again,
Jumping, leaping with
All my might and all my heart.
And the one time I thought I could reach it,
They'd moved it up to fifteen feet.
Some people call that mark
Freedom.

Don't Be a Bystander

The bully became normalized

As more and more of them

Emerged from the ground

Saturated in subconscious

Anger and hatred.

It's when the victim reaches

Their breaking point,

That the gasps of shock

And whispers of worry

Arise from the thick smoke

That masked them before.

Every once in a while

Someone might actually

Shout and say "This is wrong!"

But days later, the smoke comes

Back, and before the gasps

And whispers return,

The victim has gone missing

From their lives.

Had one of them kept talking

And used their voice,

They'd still be alive.

The Friend Whose Name I Forgot

You'd think by two months
I'd know your name.
I mean, I've called you a friend
For just as long,
But I forgot your name.
You'll have to forgive me;
Is it even appropriate for
Me to ask when
We've shared so many
Lunches together?
Maybe I'll just wait
Until someone calls your name.
Even though I don't know your name,
Just know that I have your back.

The Chains We Wear

I'm a slave to society

And ignorance

And hatred

And you?

You're a slave

To stupidity

And to fear

And to pride

Let us all break free

Of the chains

That tie us down

Are You Okay?

When they ask
"Are you okay?"
Do they really mean it?
I say I'm fine,
But if I were being real,
I'd say,
"Well, I'm clumsy,
I'm loud,
I'm sad sometimes,
Happy and excited other times
Proud that I've got a few
Good years behind me
And even more ahead."
I'm angry about all the
Terrible things going on
In this world…
I could go on,
But I know nobody cares
So I say that I'm fine
With a smile on my face.

Who Am I?

I was supposed to
Be this, I was supposed to
Be that...
Turns out
I'm supposed to be
A lot of things
I'm simply not.

Dreams vs. Reality

Don't you hate it

When you fall asleep

And you dream that

Everything you want

You have

And when you wake up

Everything slips from your fingertips

Like ice cold water

Between your fingers

The sting bringing

You back to your reality

Pale Hands

I hear the same story
Over and over and over again
About how black people are hated
We're hated because
Of the amount of melanin in our skin
How bizarre is that?
Then we're silenced by pale hands
Covering our mouths
And stealing our ability to breathe

My Mirror and I

I walk along a rocky road;

It's a winding road.

I make a turn

And, just like that,

My feet don't move anymore.

My eyes just stare at the reflective rectangle

In front of my face.

As I look into the mirror,

I am reminded of the obvious:

I'm black.

I'm different than other people.

They will first see the colour

Of my skin and judge me

From the outside,

Not by what's within.

I wonder when I will

Be considered human,

Not just black.

Fairytales

Once upon a time
Teardrops became
As normal and
As regular for me
As sunshine in California
In all honesty
They still are at times
But I know that my
Happily ever after
Is going to be just that
Happy
The word reminds me of honey—
Sweet, and something you hope
Will stick with you at all times
Maybe one day I'll
Be able to say that
I got to live
My happily ever after
 ...happily

Black Storybook

Being black is
sometimes like
Being in a time loop.
Black girls without
Fathers. Or brothers.
One's dead, the other's in jail
Because of a failed system.
Go back 50 years earlier and
The story is just the same.
It just has different names.

Save Your Tears

Don't waste your tears

On empty sadness

Save them for victory

Save them for pain and loss

Save them to cry

For the people who can't

Save them for when you fall in love

Tears are a gift

Don't waste them

Cage Fight

On the outside

You see me

My skin, my hair, my face

My body

But when you see

My outward appearance

Are you really seeing *me?*

What's on the inside

Is a beating heart

Within it is a cage

With thick black bars

Within those square walls

Are two bears

One's a gentle panda

The other is a fierce grizzly

And their fight is

A tense war

Between kindness

And aggression

Generosity

I welcomed you

With a smile

I gave you food off my table

And a place to rest

I gave you the clothes off

My very back

And yet

You still speak with

Your tongues of fiery hatred

Your eyes devil red

And when I ask you why

You can give no answer

To satisfy me

After all I've done for you

Worth

One day it'll be worth it

Worth the fight

Worth the pain

Worth the fatigue

Worth the hunger

Worth the tears

Worth it all

I'll wait and

I'll work hard

Until then

Escaping Reality

I locked myself
In the walls of
My daydream because
Reality became too much to bear

Beast

I've been trying to

Find the beauty

In the beast

Just so I don't have to

Hide it anymore

The Darkness Within

I wanted to scream
I wanted to shout
But I bit my tongue
And let the darkness of
Silence overtake me

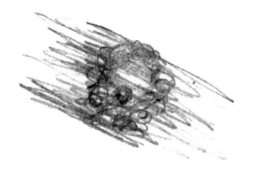

Chapter 4:
Blossoming

Beautiful Girl

"You're not that pretty."

What do you mean?

I'm gorgeous.

I was born beautiful.

See the golden

Flakes in my dark skin;

See the sparkle in my eyes;

See the smile I share with everyone.

I'm not pretty?!

Of course I am.

Black girls slay!

Diamond in the Rough

I can never be broken
You know how they say
Pressure creates diamonds?
My body is made of millions
Of them, and anything they
Try to break me down with
Gets destroyed in turn
I'm protected by my strength
And by God's grace
And by people who love me

Good Vibrations

I lower myself into the water

One foot, two foot

One thigh, other thigh

I take a deep breath

Let my worries dissipate

Chest in the water

Look at the light of the moon

See it reflecting in the water

Float on my back now

Can't hear a sound

Take a moment to think

Remember to laugh

And now laugh out loud

Like the bubbles that I breathe out now

My head under water

I see colours

Before it was all grey

Black and white

These colours are vibrant

They are square, rectangular

Triangular, beautiful colours

Like my mother's smile

They comfort me

Coloured rocks, pretty rocks

Like everything else in the world
Fish swim by, two by two

Love, love, oh love
Giving off vibrations
Of joy

Success Is Not a Ladder

I had once thought of

success as a ladder

The rungs already attached

Well, I was wrong

It's more like a river

That leads to a larger ocean

Of success

Jagged rocks of anger

Stick up everywhere

Wanting to

Cut through old wounds

Before you even get on the river

You have to build

Your own raft

Craft your own oars

You can forget about

The life jacket?

It's sink or swim

And everyone, everyone

Is going to try and drown you

Say "you're stupid"

Say "you'll never be enough"

Say "you're not pretty enough"

Say "you'll never get anywhere in life"

They'll try to destroy your raft

And take away your oars
So you go off course
But with ambition and drive
You'll succeed
You'll make it
And so will I

My Beauty's Been Earned

You can't tell me
I'm not beautiful—
I've earned every single
Stripe I have.
See my scars?
They're healed battle wounds.
I work hard
And expect nothing less
Of myself.
I promised myself
I'd leave this world
A better place
Than the one I came into.
I knew the dangers
That lurked before me.
You can't tell me
I'm not beautiful.
If my strength scares you,
It's because it should,
Because I am
A Goddess!
A Warrior!
A Queen!
The love of my life!
I am courage;
I am power.

No —you can't tell me

I'm not beautiful.

The Light She Gives

I wasn't sure how much
Longer I was going
To be able to hold on
The black gas filled the air
Infected my lungs
And I let it in
Even as it blocked
My airway
I was giving up
When a knock came at my door
And a beautiful face poked in
The crack
Letting the light in
And I had hope again
She'd saved me again
And she didn't even know it
As long as I have her
I can never give up hope

Watch Me Burn

I used to be afraid

To light the fire

Within myself

Afraid to let them

See me burn

My passion fully visible

But that was

Some time ago

Now I am the fire

And all I do

Is burn

*I'm*possible

I'm desperate to make

Something out of myself

Because I was told

That I was nothing,

And instead of accepting that,

I decided to make a big something

Out of nothing.

Some may have said

"It's impossible."

But at one point, so were we.

The Warrior in Me

I got all the tears out
Beforehand
I let them flow like a river
I was getting ready to
Push myself to
My breaking point
And then
Push myself even further
I learned a long time ago
That sometimes you have to
Go through hell to remind yourself
That there are things
Worth living for
Things worth fighting for
That's how I became a warrior
I had no choice
I had to

The Hummingbird's Garden

When the summer comes,

Grandma gives me lessons

On the types of flowers.

She picks a few

For her vibrant garden,

With the sound of the

honeybees and hummingbirds

Moving through her mind.

She shows me the ballerina flowers

And the bleeding heart flowers

And the birds of paradise.

She picks the ones that will thrive in

Her garden's environment.

She chooses what to give them,

Carefully, thoughtfully.

When I watch her,

I'm reminded of how much care

And thought she puts into me.

I'm like a flower, and she showers me with her love.

Grandma's Kitchen

When Grandma cooks a meal,

I always try to help.

But even when asking if she needs help,

I know what the answer will be:

There's only room for one person

In my kitchen. Me.

And I always end up chuckling

And letting her know that if she needed

Me, I'm there for her.

I like setting the table

For us to eat together.

My favourite part about

Eating at Grandma's house

Is that everything seems to

Taste better, because

Everyone is happy,

And because she puts love

Into whatever she makes.

Herstory

My only hope for tomorrow
Is that I become a better
Version of who I am today,
A better of version of
Who I was yesterday.
I hope I make mistakes today;
I hope I fail today;
I hope I learn today
From each mistake,
Each failure,
Because tomorrow
I'll have to look in the mirror.
I don't want to see the
Ghost of who I am now—
Only the shadow.
I know that when
I see my reflection tomorrow,
I can only become
Stronger, kinder, better
Than I am today.

Happiness

There are so many things

That make the heart swell

Things that make the heart grow

The laugh of a baby

Kisses from a puppy

The warmth of the sun

On your skin on

A summer's day

The crinkles and lines

You get when you

Have spent hours

Of your life

With a smile

Allow your heart

To fill with joy

And laughter

It will only bring you

Love and happiness

Life Is a Blessing

Blessed

The only way I could

Describe my life

Every day

Is a chance to become

Stronger and to

Better myself

I thank God

For every day

I have on this earth

God's Art

One of the most

Beautiful and magical

Creations made

Was that of the

Human body

Specifically women's bodies

It's as if God

Sculpted us from

The strongest, hardest marble

Then softened us with

Femininity, and let

Us define exactly what

Femininity means

Welcome to High School

That embarrassing thing you

Said to your crush?

It wasn't a dream.

That was high school.

Stayed up till 1 am to write

Study notes for someone else

And they didn't use them?

Welcome to high school.

The cardboard with cheese on it

That they call pizza?

It's high school.

That one person that's

Wants to be better than you,

Who turns *everything* into a competition?

That's your friendly high school nemesis.

The power-hungry teacher,

Who's out to get you?

They want you to inherit their hate

For high school.

Don't worry; these could still

Be the best years of your life...

In God's Arms

I wanted to put

My trust in Him

But the battle within me

That I thought I was facing alone

Was too much to bear

So I ran away from Him

His arms faded into memory

I sprinted as far away as I could

But I came to a cliff

I stood on the edge

Wondering if I should jump

If I had come this far

He wouldn't save me

I had gone against Him

The ground began to shake

And I felt the earth

Give way beneath me

And I prepared for my death

But arms wrapped around me

In a loving embrace

And I stopped fighting

And sunk into the contours

Of His arms and knew that in any battle

I would never be alone

He would always be by my side

My Best Friend Lily

Sometimes I need
A break from humans
A break from the pressure
Of societal expectations
And it's the fur I feel
Caressing my bare hands
That reminds me I'm
Not alone
When Lily gives me
A kiss on the cheek
With her warm,
Unspoken love
I know I am part of
A friendship that
No human could ever
But she does
Every footstep I take
Is matched by her paws
Prancing beside me
Dogs provide a connections
That go beyond the
Ones humans can

Being Myself

The confidence I feel
When I pick out an
Outfit that's colourful,
When I slip on my platform shoes,
And when I form my curls
Into perfect ringlets,
The confidence I feel
Is unbeatable.
When I put work into
My mental health,
And when I make the
Ones I adore smile,
My confidence skyrockets.
I'm most confident
Just being me.

Disneyland

The smiles that refused
To leave our faces
As we put our hands up
And screamed over the hills and bumps
The roller coaster raced around.
The magic of that place was
Unmatched, grasping its
Willing victims in
A hug of joy, and happiness.
The princes, and princesses,
The mice and the ducks —
We saw them all
The thrill coursed through
Our veins and we celebrated
A vacation that had brought us
Even closer together.
We carried the laughs, smiles,
And fun from Disneyland
Back home.

Meditation

It slowed my heart
And my mind
To breathe slowly
To release the stress
And breathe in peace

True Beauty

If I could show her
Who I am now,
She would be so proud.
I would be her inspiration.
My strength has only grown
Since I've become myself.
Do I have it all figured out?
No, but I have goals and dreams
And a future that is uninterrupted
By embarrassment or complete and
Utter self-doubt
If she could see me now,
That high school girl,
She'd see that I laugh
Real, genuine laughter.
She'd see that I love,
And that despite everything,
I've become unstoppable.
If she could see me now,
She'd understand what
True beauty is.

Reminiscing

Grandma rides in the backseat

Beside me, for our snowy adventure.

Going to the nature park

Geared up in winter boots

And tightly wrapped scarves and jackets,

We walk together,

Holding each other

And admiring the white snow

Blanketing the cedars and the Douglas firs.

Our footprints leave a

Temporary tattoo, showing us

That we were here together

Laughing and enjoying ourselves.

Pain Does Not Discriminate

He dropped another
Coin into the black box
Then sealed it up,
Knowing that no matter
How heavy it got,
He would never be able to
Empty it.
He'd tried peering into
The coin slot
To see just what was
Weighing it down,
But all he could see
Was pure darkness.
In his small office,
He sits in his corner
In his brown leather chair,
An identical one sat across
From his.
For years, he'd waited
For someone to rest in it,
But no one did
He wanted to tell
Someone about the black box
And how it had plagued him.
His fear was that

He'd take that pain
To his grave.
He knew that if he revealed
To anyone the depression,
He faced, and the fear
He faced, and why all
Of those feelings had arisen,
No one would believe him.
So he shut out those emotions,
Until, one day, a person
Came and sat in the
Brown leather chair,
The one that had never been occupied,
And listened to him
Dumping each coin from
The black box
Leaving the man
With internal peace.

I Love Myself

I spent nearly two decades
Of my life worried
About who I was and
Whether I was fitting in
With other people
Who weren't like me
I didn't like my clothes
So I wore theirs
I didn't like my skin
So I shed mine
And used theirs
Spoiler alert: they didn't fit me
I didn't like me
So I changed in order
To fit in
Then I thought
Maybe I wasn't meant to fit in
Blend in,
Be in.
I was born to be different
Not to be like everyone else
I was meant to be the blue fish
Swimming in a school of orange fish
I spent a part of
My life trying to be someone else
Or really,

Anyone but me
And along the way I learned
Why it is so important
To love yourself

Black Goddess

Beautiful white teeth

Stunning melanin

You are a black goddess

Smooth curves

Full lips

Glistening golden skin

You are a black goddess

Powerful words

Battle scars

You're a black warrior

Hold your head high

Beautiful black girl

I Am Woman

When I was born

I had no clue

That because I didn't

Have physical balls

I was going to be treated differently

And seen differently

And viewed as inadequate

For being a girl

Well, people

It takes real balls to

Go through what I've been through

Through things women

Have been dealing with for centuries

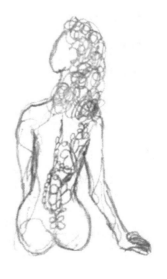

My Garden

My garden has been with me

Since the day I was born.

Seeds were planted

And since then, I've been taking

Care of my garden as best I can.

I love the beautiful flowers

That fill the air with pleasant smells.

I love the roses with their thorns.

Some of the dark green vines

Have become overgrown,

I've got to look after those more.

I water my garden every day

To help them thrive.

I even water it when it's raining,

And sometimes that makes them

Nearly drown.

When you look at your garden,

Make sure you care for it.

Let it prosper,

And you will prosper in turn.

A Love Letter to Vancouver Island

Minutes from the ocean

Seconds from a climb

On a high mountain

Trees to get lost in

And wildlife to admire

Vancouver Island truly is

A slice of heaven on earth

Miles from a city

With vibrant people

Sun in the summer

Snow in the winter

It all makes me pause

And appreciate my home

Rainbows

Droplets of water

Bathed by sunlight;

When the light touches them,

The colours are revealed.

People are so similar to

The rainbows we admire on

Those damp and sunny days.

Like the water droplets, we are

Unnoticeable to one another,

But when the light touches us at

The right time angle,

Our beauty and uniqueness are

Revealed to the world.

You Are a Diamond

You don't need to be

Famous or rich to make

A difference in the world.

As long as you share the good

You have in your heart,

You let the world shine

Bright like the diamond you are.

The Birth of a Goddess

What created the

Burning pit in my stomach

Wasn't the people

Who chucked basketballs

At my head

Just to see if it would hurt;

It wasn't the ones who

Told me to scrub the dirt off;

It wasn't the ones who asked me

Why I was so dark.

I just used them

As an excuse, an easy explanation.

No—what really ate me up

Inside, what really made my

Stomach burn, was when

She asked me if I loved myself

And I couldn't say yes.

The self-hate choked

Me from behind,

So I couldn't face it,

I couldn't see it.

My biggest bullies

Weren't the ones from my past;

My biggest bully was my mind.

And I knew that. I knew

It had been a long time

Since I'd cared about what

People thought.

But to think my mind

Was my enemy

Was just too much.

I knew their ignorance was

Their burden, not mine;

I knew that years ago.

I was a bully to myself

And I had to fix it.

It took years,

But I've learned

To love myself in all my glory.

Goddesses aren't created overnight—

They earn that title.

Exhibit of Joy

Hold onto the bus pole

Grandma said.

We were going on an adventure.

This was my first time riding a bus,

And Grandma and I were

Going to the museum downtown.

We were dressed in dressy, but comfy outfits.

Grandma always dresses nicely.

When I was younger I called her spicy,

Because of her stylish clothes.

Today, we were looking at

The Mayan exhibit.

We both love learning new things,

And discovering worlds we didn't

Really know existed.

We walked through the exhibit together.

Admiring the art and the history

That was being stored in the maze

Of the Mayan wonders of the past.

It was a day I'll never forget.

If I were to put snapshots of my happiest

Memories on display,

Grandma would be in all of them.

If you walked through my

Exhibit of joy I've experienced,

You would see me shopping with

Grandma, listening to music with her,

Going on walks where we just

Enjoyed each other's company.

You'd see the meals we shared,

The lessons she taught me,

And the love we have for each other.

That's the exhibit I want to share,

The art of my life of joy.

The Hummingbird's Song

Grandma taught me how

To feed the hummingbirds.

She told me if I put out

The feeder,

The hummingbirds would come.

When I checked on the feeders,

That's when I saw him:

A beautiful Rufous hummingbird.

He was so pretty, flitting about,

It's wings beating fast, yet gracefully.

In my head, I wondered if he could sing.

I admired his grace as he explored

My garden, and flew back

To the feeder.

Then he began to sing.

The high-pitched chirps of his song

Filled the air,

And I listened,

The melody drawing me into

The beauty of his aura.

I thought about Grandma,

Teaching me how to attract the birds,

And I smiled as I listened

To the hummingbird's song.

Building My Own Table

There have been so many

People wanting a seat

At this table,

Wanting to be heard.

And when it was my turn,

I noticed there wasn't a seat for me.

I figured, the table was old,

It needed a serious update.

So I built a bigger table.

One that could expand, as more people

Joined us.

Then I built new chairs,

And added five more around the table,

So that when the next people came,

Their seats would be ready.

Being heard would no longer

Be a privilege.

Family

My parents always told me that
Family was the most important thing
In the whole world.
When I think of happiness,
I think of dancing with Mom.
I think of painting with Dad.
I think of listening to
The songs my brother has written.
When I think of happiness,
I think of the times
Mom's eaten my culinary creations,
And told me they were good
Even when they were terrible.
I think of Dad building with me.
I think of my brother
Making me laugh,
Even when he doesn't try to.
When I think of family,
I think of how lucky I am to
Be loved, and the fact that I'll never
Have to face challenges in life alone.

Uncle John

A couple months ago,

There you were,

Smiling and laughing

With us all.

To some, you may

Just be a memory

But to us, you are

The warm hugs

The belly laughs

The infectious smiles

That will forever

Remain in our hearts.

Though the road to healing

Will be long

For us all,

You will always be there

To embrace us with

Your welcoming arms.

Up to this point

I have only known life with you

And the change saddens me

But I know that you are still

With us

Thank you for the joy

And comfort

You brought to us all

Acknowledgements

First, I want to say thank you to my Mom and Dad, who have supported me all my life. You have been present for every adventure and encouraged me to chase my dreams and fulfill my goals. I wouldn't have been able to complete this book had it not been for your enthusiasm and support. Thank you, Mom, for giving me the courage to learn a new drawing style, add my own illustrations in my book, and encouraging me to embrace self publishing. Thank you to my Dad for always drawing and painting with me for my entire life. You inspire me to do my best in everything I do. I love you both so much. I am so fortunate to have parents that have supported me.

I'd also like to thank my (little) brother for your contributions, reading my poems, and offering your feedback. You are the best! You've helped bring this book to life and you've been so supportive throughout the process.

A huge thank you to my Aunty Jill for telling me about the poetry workshop that inspired me to write this book. Without you, this book would never have happened. Thank you for reigniting my passion for poetry.

www.ingramcontent.com/pod-product-compliance
Lightning Source LLC
LaVergne TN
LVHW011318260125
802190LV00002B/271